what matters now
things to think about and do this year

This is an authorized hard copy of *What Matters Now*, which was conceived and edited by Seth Godin. Seth and his team of authors haven't proofread or approved this physical edition, so layout decisions belong to the publishers. Thanks for reading!

What Matters Now is copyright 2010 by its respective authors:
Seth Godin, Anne Jackson, Jessica Hagy, Jacqueline Novogratz, Hugh MacLeod, Elizabeth Gilbert, Howard Mann, Chris Meyer, Michael Hyatt, Rajesh Setty, Jackie Huba, Ben McConnell, Mark Hurst, Chris Anderson, Tom Peters, William C. Taylor, Marti Barletta, John Wood, Alan M. Webber, Daniel H. Pink, Tony Hsieh, Dave Ramsey, Saul Griffith, Jeffrey Pfeffer, Jack Covert, Sally Haldorson, Steven Pressfield, Guy Kawasaki, Mitch Joel, Alisa Miller, Clay Johnson, Piers Fawkes, Karen Armstrong, Joichi Ito, Megan Casey, Jay Parkinson, Robyn Waters, Dave Balter, Micah Sifry, George Dyson, Carne Ross, Gary Vaynerchuk, David Meerman Scott, Jeff Jonas, Chip and Dan Heath, Derek Sivers, Fred Krupp, Tim Sanders, Fred Wilson, Kevin Kelly, Phoebe Espiritu, Aaron Wall, Sally Hogshead, David Weinberger, Martha Beck, John Moore, Todd Sattersten, Chimamanda Ngozi Adichie, Paco Underhill, Mark Rovner, Dale Dougherty, Gina Trapani, Michael Schrage
 Ramit Sethi, Lisa Gansky, Merlin Mann, Dan Ariely, Penelope Trunk, Jason Fried, Arianna Huffington, Dan Roam, Tim O'Reilly, J.C. Hutchins, and Aimee Johnson.
All rights reserved.

Room to Read® is a registered trademark of Room to Read.

Original Ebook editing and coordination by Ishita Gupta.

Hard copy conceived and coordinated by Bernadette Jiwa - www.questionsfornow.com

Cover and book design by Paul Durban - www.blazonfire.com

Published by Triiibes Press

ISBN 978-0-557-25576-4

All proceeds from the sale of
What Matters Now go to Room to Read.®

Room to Read®

Room to Read® is an innovative non-profit leader dedicated to promoting and enabling global education. Founded in 2000, the organization is based on the belief that education is crucial to breaking the cycle of poverty in the developing world. Since then, the organization has supported over three million children by providing better access to higher-quality educational opportunities.

Room to Read® has established more than 800 schools and over 7,500 bilingual libraries with six million books, and continues to support the education of more than 8,700 girls. Room to Read® is providing opportunities that change children's lives and communities throughout Bangladesh, Cambodia, India, Laos, Nepal, South Africa, Sri Lanka, Vietnam and Zambia.

By 2010, Room to Read® hopes to improve literacy for five million children by establishing over 10,000 libraries and distributing nearly nine million children's books. For more information visit our website at www.roomtoread.org.

here's what we're working on and thinking about.

what about you?

generosity

When the economy tanks, it's natural to think of yourself first. You have a family to feed a mortgage to pay. Getting more appears to be the order of business.

It turns out that the connected economy doesn't respect this natural instinct. Instead, we're rewarded for being generous. Generous with our time and money but most important
generous with our art.

If you make a difference, people will gravitate to you. They want to engage, to interact and to get you more involved.

In a digital world, the gift I give you almost always benefits me more than it costs.

If you make a difference, you also make a connection. You interact with people who want to be interacted with and you make changes that people respect and yearn for.

Art can't happen without someone who seeks to make a difference. This is your art, it's what you do. You touch people or projects and change them for the better.

This year, you'll certainly find that the more you give the more you get.

Seth Godin is a blogger and speaker. His new book, *Linchpin*, comes out in January.

fear

Have you ever wondered who's behind that little voice in your head that tells you, "you're in this by yourself, one person doesn't make a difference, so why even try?"

His name is Fear. Fear plays the role of antagonist in the story of your life. You must rid yourself of him using all necessary means.

We're often impressed by those who appear to be fearless. The people who fly to the moon. Chase tornadoes. Enter dangerous war zones. Skydive. Speak in front of thousands of people. Stand up to cancer. Raise money and adopt a child that isn't their flesh and blood. So, why are we so inspired by them? Because deep down, we are them. We all share the same characteristics. We're all divinely human. Until Fear is gone, (and realize he may never completely leave) make the decision to be courageous. The world needs your story in order to be complete.

Anne Jackson blogs, tweets, and writes books. Her most recent work, *Permission To Speak Freely: Essays and Art on Fear, Confession and Grace,* will be available in August.

facts

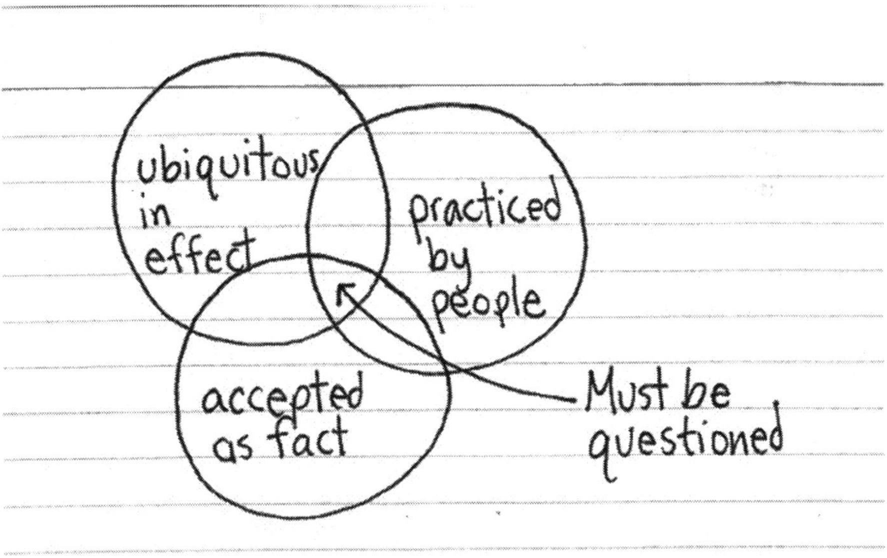
ubiquitous in effect
practiced by people
accepted as fact
Must be questioned

Jessica Hagy blogs at thisisindexed.com and is the author of a wonderful book called *Indexed*.

dignity

Dignity is more important than wealth. It's going to be a long, long time before we can make everyone on Earth wealthy, but we can help people find dignity this year (right now if we choose to).

Dignity comes from creating your own destiny and from the respect you get from your family, your peers and society.

A farmer able to feed his family and earn enough to send his kids to school has earned the respect of the people in his village—and more important, a connection to the rest of us.

It's easy to take dignity away from someone, but difficult to give it to them. The last few years have taught us just how connected the entire world is—a prostitute in the slums of Nairobi is just as important a figure in your life as the postman in the next town. And in a world where everything is connected, the most important thing we can do is treat our fellows with dignity.

Giving a poor person food or money might help them survive another day… but it doesn't give them dignity. There's a better way.

Creating ways for people to solve their own problems isn't just an opportunity in 2010. It is an obligation.

Jacqueline Novogratz is the founder of the Acumen Fund and author of *The Blue Sweater.*

meaning

Sing in your own voice. Don't worry about finding inspiration. It comes eventually. BEING POOR SUCKS.
EVERYBODY HAS THEIR OWN PRIVATE MOUNT EVEREST THEY WERE PUT ON THIS EARTH TO CLIMB.
Start blogging. The choice of media is irrelevant. Write from the heart.
THE BEST WAY TO GET APPROVAL IS NOT TO NEED IT.
Don't try to stand out from the crowd; avoid crowds altogether. SAVOR OBSCURITY WHILE IT LASTS.
You are responsible for your own experience. Power is never given. Nobody cares.
Whatever choice you make, The Devil gets his due eventually. Power is taken. Do it for yourself.
BEWARE OF TURNING HOBBIES INTO JOBS. Worrying about "Commercial vs. Artistic" is a complete waste of time.
Merit can be bought. Passion can't. When your dreams become reality, they are no longer your dreams.
allow your work to age with you. If you accept the pain,
Keep your day job. ignore everybody. it cannot hurt you.
Don't worry about finding inspiration. It comes eventually.
Remain frugal. Dying young is overrated.
If your biz plan depends on you suddenly being "discovered" by some big shot, your plan will probably fail.
NEVER COMPARE YOUR INSIDE WITH SOMEBODY ELSE'S OUTSIDE.
THE MOST IMPORTANT THING A CREATIVE PERSON CAN LEARN PROFESSIONALLY
IS WHERE TO DRAW THE RED LINE THAT SEPARATES WHAT YOU ARE WILLING TO DO, AND WHAT YOU ARE NOT.
Everyone is born creative; everyone is given a box of crayons in kindergarten.
Companies that squelch creativity can no longer compete with companies that champion creativity.
The hardest part of being creative is getting used to it.
Selling out is harder than it looks. You have to find your own schtick.
The world is changing AVOID THE WATERCOOLER GANG. Put the hours in.
Meaning Scales, People Don't. The more talented somebody is, the less they need the props.

@hugh

Hugh MacLeod blogs at gapingvoid.com and is author of *Ignore Everybody*.

ease

We are the strivingest people who have ever lived. We are ambitious, time-starved, competitive, distracted. We move at full velocity, yet constantly fear we are not doing enough. Though we live longer than any humans before us, our lives feel shorter, restless, breathless...

Dear ones, EASE UP. Pump the brakes. Take a step back. Seriously. Take two steps back. Turn off all your electronics and surrender over all your aspirations and do absolutely nothing for a spell. I know, I know – we all need to save the world. But trust me: The world will still need saving tomorrow.

In the meantime, you're going to have a stroke soon (or cause a stroke in somebody else) if you don't calm the hell down. So go take a walk. Or don't. Consider actually exhaling. Find a body of water and float. Hit a tennis ball against a wall. Tell your colleagues that you're off meditating (people take meditation seriously, so you'll be absolved from guilt) and then actually, secretly, nap.

My radical suggestion? Cease participation, if only for one day this year – if only to make sure that we don't lose forever the rare and vanishing human talent of appreciating ease.

Elizabeth Gilbert is the author of *Eat, Pray, Love*. Her new book, *Committed: A Skeptic Makes Peace With Marriage,* will be published in January, 2010.

connected

There are tens of thousands of businesses making many millions a year in profits that still haven't ever heard of Twitter, blogs or Facebook. Are they all wrong? Have they missed out or is the joke really on us? They do business through personal relationships, by delivering great customer service and it's working for them. They're more successful than most of those businesses who spend hours pontificating about how others lose out by missing social media and the latest wave. And yet they're doing business. Great business. Not writing about it. Doing it.

I'm continually amazed by the number of people on Twitter and on blogs, and the growth of people (and brands) on Facebook. But I'm also amazed by how so many of us are spending our time. The echo chamber we're building is getting larger and louder.

More megaphones don't equal a better dialogue. We've become slaves to our mobile devices and the glow of our screens. It used to be much more simple and, somewhere, simple turned into slow.

We walk the streets with our heads down staring into 3-inch screens while the world whisks by doing the same. And yet we're convinced we are more connected to each other than ever before. Multi-tasking has become a badge of honor. I want to know why.

I don't have all the answers to these questions but I find myself thinking about them more and more. In between tweets, blog posts and Facebook updates.

Howard Mann is a speaker, entrepreneur and the author of *Your Business Brickyard*.

re-capitalism

Capitalism is not immutable—it's changed before (remember industrializations?) and will again.

Darwin wrote about the finches of the Galapagos Islands, observing that the shape of each population's beaks matched the form of the particular flowers that provided their food. Think of business as the individuals of the capitalist species. **The shape of companies will evolve as the world changes around them.**

What changes? Two big ones: **The world's growth will no longer come from the high-income economies** (they consume 77% of the world GDP today—only 32% by 2050.) Second, just as industrial technology shaped the society of the United States' in the 20th Century, **information technology will be the basis of the emerging "digital wave" economies in the 21st.** Like finches businesses will change their shapes to make their living in this new low income, high growth, globally connected, information-intensive environment.

How? They will learn to price and market goods whose marginal cost is zero. They will learn to profit from giving value away. They will prefer collaboration to competition. They will assume responsibility for the newly measurable "externalities" they impose on their societies.

If you live or operate in the developed world, you've got a problem—**you have a lot to unlearn, and no short-term incentive to do it. But better not ignore the competitor with the strange looking beak.**

Chris Meyer, co-author of *Blur, The Speed of Change in the Connected Economy*, is writing a book about the evololution of capitalism.

vision

Vision is the lifeblood of any organization. It is what keeps it moving forward. It provides meaning to the day-to-day challenges and setbacks that make up the rumble and tumble of real life.

In a down economy—particularly one that has taken most of us by surprise—things get very tactical. We are just trying to survive. What worked yesterday does not necessarily work today. What works today may not necessarily work tomorrow. Decisions become pragmatic.

But after a while this wears on people. They don't know why their efforts matter. They cannot connect their actions to a larger story. Their work becomes a matter of just going through the motions, living from weekend to weekend, paycheck to paycheck. This is where great leadership makes all the difference.

Leadership is more than influence. It is about reminding people of what it is we are trying to build—and why it matters. It is about painting a picture of a better future. It comes down to pointing the way and saying, "C'mon. We can do this!"

When times are tough, vision is the first casualty. Before conditions can improve, it is the first thing we must recover.

Michael Hyatt is the CEO of Thomas Nelson Publishers. He blogs on "Leading with Purpose" at MichaelHyatt.com and also Twitters at @MichaelHyatt.

enrichment

We are all on a search – a search for more meaning in our lives. Through choosing to enrich other people's lives, you add meaning to both their life and your own. Some simple steps to follow:

1. Commit: Commit to lifetime-relationships that span events, companies, causes and geographic boundaries.

2. Care: Care for the concerns of others as if they are your own.

3. Connect: Aim to connect those who will benefit and enrich each other's lives in equal measure.

4. Communicate: Communicate candidly. Tell people what they should hear rather than what they want to hear.

5. Expand Capacity: Aim to expand people's capacity to help them give and get more from their own lives.

The Litmus Test: If you are truly enriching someone's life, they will typically miss you in their past. They think their lives would have been even better if they had met you earlier. You are only as rich as the enrichment you bring to the world around you.

Rajesh Setty is an entrepreneur, author and speaker based in Silicon Valley. He blogs at LifeBeyondCode.com.

1%

Two tech executives with no food experience and no marketing budget launch a product called Bacon Salt. Next, they search for people on social networking sites who profess a love for bacon, then friend them. Among a small percentage of those people, enthusiasm begins to spread about Bacon Salt. What began as a tribe quickly multiplies into 37,000 fans on Facebook and MySpace.

Months later, the buzz spills over into newspaper articles, TV interviews and the holy grail of PR, an appearance on Oprah. Two guys who knew nothing about the food business and had no marketing budget now had a certifiable cult hit. Inspired, they create several other bacon-flavored products. It's the birth of a brand.

Their success began with a small – very small – group of self-identified fans of a category. Even if social networks have millions of members, it will never translate into millions of buzz-spreaders. The Bacon Salt story illustrates that it's usually a small percentage of the tribe within the larger tribe who spread the word—usually about 1 percent. They are the One Percenters.

The One Percenters are not the usual suspects of name-brand tech bloggers, mommy bloggers and or business bloggers. The One Percenters are often hidden in the crevices of niches, yet they are the roots of word of mouth. This year, your job is to find them and attract them.

Jackie Huba and **Ben McConnell** are the authors of the books *Citizen Marketers* and *Creating Customer Evangelists*. They blog at Church of the Customer (churchofthecustomer.com).

speaking

Speaking soon? Keep this in mind: people at events are hungry for authenticity. Saying something you might not have said elsewhere is a good way to find your authentic voice.

For my own conference, I often give advice to speakers before they come on stage. Here's an exercise for anyone who wants to connect with an audience. A few weeks before the event, when you start preparing the talk, write out everything you spend your time doing - professional work, side projects at home, everything.

Now pick the one thing you're most excited about. Now consider: why is that so important to you? Design your talk from that point, as if you started by saying, "My name is X, and I'm passionate about XYZ because…" The rest of your talk should fall into place easily enough.

Yes, it's important to know your audience, use A/V materials wisely, watch your time, and so on. But you have to build the talk around your passion.

Here's the final measure of your success as a speaker: did you change something? Are attendees leaving with a new idea, some new inspiration, perhaps a renewed commitment to their work or to the world? Be honest, be authentic, and speak from your passion. Yes, it means taking a risk. But the results might surprise you.

Mark Hurst runs Gel (gelconference.com) and founded Creative Good, a customer experience consultancy.

atoms

The past decade has been an extraordinary adventure in discovering new social models on the Web—ways to work, create and organize outside of the traditional institutions of companies, governments and academia. But the next decade will be all about applying these models to the real world. Atoms are the new bits!

Just take one example: making stuff. The Internet democratized publishing, broadcasting and communications, and the consequence was a massive increase in the range of both participants and participation in everything digital—the long tail of bits. Now the same is happening to manufacturing—the long tail of things.

The tools of factory production, from electronics assembly to 3D printing, are now available to individuals, in batches as small as a single unit. Anybody with an idea and little bit of self-taught expertise can set assembly lines in China into motion with a few keystrokes. A few days later, a prototype will be at their door, and it all checks out, they can push a few more buttons and be in full production. They are a virtual microfactory, able to design and sell goods without any infrastructure or even inventory; everything is assembled and drop-shipped by the contractors, who can serve hundreds of such small customers simultaneously.

Today, there are microfactories making everything from cars to bike parts to local cabinetmakers with computer-controlled routers making bespoke furniture in any design you can imagine. The collective potential of a million garage tinkerers is now about to be unleashed on the global markets, as ideas go straight into entrepreneurship, no tooling required. "Three guys with laptops" used to describe a web startup. Now it describes a hardware company, too. Peer production, open source, crowdsourcing, DIY and UGC—all these digital phenomena are starting to play out in the world of atoms, too. The Web was just the proof of concept. Now the revolution gets real.

Chris Anderson is Editor in Chief of Wired Magazine, and the author of *The Long Tail* and *FREE*. He also runs a micromanfacturing robotics company at diydrones.com.

excellence

The 19 Es of Excellence.

Enthusiasm! Be an irresistible force of nature! **Exuberance!** Vibrate—cause earthquakes! **Execution!** Do it! Now! Get it done! Barriers are baloney! Excuses are for wimps! Accountability is gospel! Adhere to the Bill Parcells doctrine: "Blame no one! Expect nothing! Do something!" **Empowerment!** Respect and appreciation rule! Always ask, "What do you think?" Then listen! Then let go and liberate! Then celebrate! **Edginess!** Perpetually dancing at the frontier, and a little or a lot beyond. **Enraged!** Determined to challenge and change the status quo! Motto: "If it ain't broke, break it!" **Engaged!** Addicted to MBWA/Managing by Wandering Around. In touch. Always. **Electronic!** Partners with the world 60/60/24/7 via electronic community building of every sort. **Encompassing!** Relentlessly pursue diverse options—the more diversity the merrier! Diversity per se "works"! **Emotion!** The alpha. The omega. The essence of leadership. The essence of sales. The essence of marketing. The essence. Period. Acknowledge it. **Empathy!** Connect, connect, connect with others' reality and aspirations! "Walk in the other person's shoes"—until the shoes have holes! **Ears!** Effective listening: Strategic Advantage Number 1! **Experience!** Life is theater! Make every activity-contact memorable! Standard: "Insanely Great"/Steve Jobs; "Radically Thrilling"/BMW. **Eliminate!** Keep it simple! **Error-prone!** Ready! Fire! Aim! Try a lot of stuff and make a lot of boo-boos and then try some more stuff and make some more boo-boos—all of it at the speed of light! **Evenhanded!** Straight as an arrow! Fair to a fault! Honest as Abe! **Expectations!** Michelangelo: "The greatest danger for most of us is not that our aim is too high and we miss it, but that it is too low and we reach it." Amen! **Eudalmonia!** Pursue the highest of human moral purpose—the core of Aristotle's philosophy. Be of service. Always. **Excellence!** Never an exception! *If not Excellence, what?*

Tom Peters blogs at tompeters.com. His new book, *The Little BIG Thing*s: *163 Ways to Pursue Excellence* will be available in March 2010.

most

Imagine any and every field possible. There are so many brands, so many choices, so many claims, so much clutter, that the central challenge is for an organization or an individual is to rise above the fray. It's not good enough anymore to be "pretty good" at everything. You have to be the most of something: the most elegant, the most colorful, the most responsive, the most accessible.

For decades, organizations and their leaders were comfortable with strategies and practices that kept them in the middle of the road—that's where the customers were, so that's what felt safe and secure.

Today, with so much change and uncertainty, so much pressure and new ways to do things, the middle of the road is the road to nowhere. As Jim Hightower, the colorful Texas populist, is fond of saying, "There's nothing in the middle of the road but yellow stripes and dead armadillos."

We might add: companies and their leaders struggling to stand out from the crowd, as they play by the same old rules in a crowded marketplace. **Are you the most of anything?**

William C. Taylor is a cofounder of Fast Company magazine. His forthcoming book is *Practically Radical*.

strengths

Forget about working on your weaknesses —> Focus on supporting your strengths. I worked on my weaknesses for 40 years to little avail. Still "needs improvement," as they say. Why? Easy. We hate doing things we're not good at, so we avoid them. No practice makes perfect hard to attain. But my strengths – ah, I love my strengths. I'll work on them till the purple cows come home. When we love what we do, we do more and more, and pretty soon we're pretty good at it. The beautiful thing about being on a team is that, believe it or not, lots of people love doing the things you hate. And hate doing the things you love. So quit diligently developing your weaknesses. Instead, partner with someone very UNlike you, share the work and share the wealth and everyone's happy. Relatedly, women are rather UNlike men and often approach problems and opportunities with a different outlook. Yet books and coaches often encourage us to adopt male strengths and, lacking understanding, to relinquish our own. The irony is, studies show that more women in leadership translates unequivocally into better business results.

Wouldn't it make more sense for both men and women to appreciate each other's strengths so we all work on what comes naturally?

Marti Barletta, speaker, consultant and author of *Marketing to Women* and *PrimeTime Women*, is currently working on her next book, *Attracting Women: Marketing Your Company to the 21st Century's Best Candidates.*

ripple

Education has a ripple effect. One drop can initiate a cascade of possibility, each concentric circle gaining in size and traveling further. If you get education right, you get many things right: escape from poverty, better family health, and improved status of women.

Educate a girl, and you educate her children and generations to follow.

Yet for hundreds of millions of kids in the developing world, the ripple never begins. Instead, there's a seemingly inescapable whirlpool of poverty. In the words of a headmaster I once met in Nepal: "We are too poor to afford education. But until we have education, we will always be poor." That's why there are 300 million children in the developing world who woke up this morning and did not go to school. And why there are over 750 million people unable to read and write, nearly 2/3 of whom are girls and women.

I dream of a world in which we've changed that. A world with thousands of new schools. Tens of thousands of new libraries. Each with equal access for all children.

The best time to plant a tree was twenty years ago. The second best time is now.

John Wood is Founder & Executive Chairman, Room to Read, which has built over 850 schools and opened over 7,500 libraries serving 3 million children. He is the author of *Leaving Microsoft to Change the World*.

unsustainability

Everyone is pursuing sustainability. But if change happens when the cost of the status quo is greater than the risk of change, we really need to focus on raising the costs of the unsustainable systems that represent the unsustainable status quo. Unsustainable failed educational systems, obesity-producing systems, energy systems, transportation systems, health care systems. Each and every one is unsustainable. It's more "innovative" to talk about bright, shiny, new sustainable systems, but before we can even work on the right side of the change equation, we need to drive up the costs of the unsustainable systems that represent the dead weight of the past.

The road to sustainability goes through a clear-eyed look at unsustainability.

Alan M. Webber is co-founding editor of Fast Company magazine and author, most recently of *Rules of Thumb: 52 Truths for Winning at Business Without Losing Yourself.*

autonomy

Management isn't natural.

I don't mean that it's weird or toxic – just that it doesn't emanate from nature. "Management" isn't a tree or a river. It's a telegraph or a transistor radio. Somebody invented it. And over time, most inventions – from the candle to the cotton gin to the compact disc – lose their usefulness.

Management is great if you want people to comply – to do specific things a certain way. But it stinks if you want people to engage – to think big or give the world something it didn't know it was missing. For creative, complex, conceptual challenges—i.e what most of us now do for a living—40 years of research in behavioral science and human motivation says that self-direction works better. And that requires autonomy. Lots of it. If we want engagement, and the mediocrity-busting results it produces, we have to make sure people have autonomy over the four most important aspects of their work:

Task – What they do. Time – When they do it. Technique – How they do it. Team – Whom they do it with.

After a decade of truly spectacular underachievement, what we need now is less management and more freedom – fewer individual automatons and more autonomous individuals.

Daniel H. Pink is the author of *A Whole New Mind*. His new book, *Drive: The Surprising Truth About What Motivates Us*, comes out in late December, 2009.

poker

BUSINESS IS A GAME. Everything I know about business I learned from poker: financials, strategy, education, and culture.

FINANCIALS: The guy who wins the most hands is not the guy who makes the most money in the long run. • The guy who never loses a hand is not the guy who makes the most money in the long run. • Go for positive expected value, not what's least risky. • You will win or lose individual hands, but it's what happens in the long term that matters.

STRATEGY: Learn to adapt. Adjust your style of play as the dynamics of the game change. • The players with the most stamina and focus usually win. • Hope is not a good plan. • Stick to your principles.

EDUCATION: Never stop learning. Read books. Learn from others who have done it before. • Learn by doing. Theory is nice, but nothing replaces actual experience. • Just because you win a hand doesn't mean you're good and you don't have more learning to do. You might have just gotten lucky.

CULTURE: To become really good, you need to live it, breathe it, and sleep it. • Be nice and make friends. It's a small community. • Have fun. The game is a lot more enjoyable when you're trying to do more than just make money.

Tony Hsieh is the CEO of Zappos.com and the author of the soon-to-be-published book *Delivering Happiness*. Tony's (longer) blog post is *Everything I Know About Business I Learned from Poker.*

momentum

Malcolm Gladwell says it takes 10,000 hours of practice to become an "Outlier." He is, of course, right. My mother says practice makes perfect. She is, of course, right. A billionaire friend once told me to read one of the best stories on successful living, The Tortoise and the Hare. He says, "Every time I read that book, the tortoise wins. Slow and steady wins the race." He is, of course, right.

Whether it is branding or wealth building, I call it The Momentum Theorem.

$$\frac{Fi}{T}(G) = M$$

FOCUSED INTENSITY over TIME multiplied by GOD equals Unstoppable Momentum. Not many people in our A.D.D. culture can stay FOCUSED, but those who can are on their way to winning. Add to the focus some serious pull-your-shirt-off-and-paint-yourself-blue-at-the-football-game INTENSITY, and now you have a person who is a difference-maker. But very few companies or people can maintain that FOCUSED INTENSITY over TIME. It takes time to be great, it takes time to create critical mass, it takes time to be an "overnight success."

Lastly, you and I are finite, while GOD is infinite. So, multiply your efforts through Him and watch the areas of your life move toward winning like never before.

Dave Ramsey is a nationally syndicated radio talk show host, best-selling author of *The Total Money Makeover*, and host of The Dave Ramsey Show on the Fox Business Network.

consequence

There is little evidence that we will solve the environmental challenges of our time. Individuals too readily allow responsibility for the solutions to fall on larger entities like governments, rather than themselves. I find one very significant reason for hope amidst this largely hopeless topic. We are learning to measure consequence. Galileo said something akin to "measure what is measurable, make measurable what is not." We are slowly gaining expertise in measuring our impact in terms of carbon, energy demand, water use, and toxicity production.

Why is this hopeful? Now that we can say definitively that even the production of a soda bottle has a measurable (if tiny) increase in greenhouse gases, it's hard for a thinking individual not to acknowledge that they are working against the things they say they want. After a century of isolating the product or service from its resulting impact, the tide is turning. We are making consequence visible. We will witness the first generation who can truly know the impact of everything they do on the ecological support systems that surround them.

My hope is that we will use this knowledge wisely. We will put aside old ideas of what is good and bad for the environment and ourselves, and will quantitatively make the changes we need with new foresight.

Saul Griffith is a MacArthur Fellow and new father who blogs at energyliteracy.com and designs solutions for climate change at otherlab.com.

power

Power provokes ambivalence. Power-seeking is politically incorrect. So power remains cloaked in mystery and emotion, the organization's last dirty secret.

John Gardner, the founder of Common Cause, noted that nothing gets done without power. Social change requires the power to mobilize resources. That's why leaders are preoccupied with power. As Michael Marmot and other epidemiological researchers show, possessing the power to control your work and social environment—having autonomy and control over your job—is one of the best predictors of health and mortality. Obtaining power requires will and skill—the ambition to do the hard work necessary, and the insight required to direct your energy productively. Power comes from an ability to build your reputation, create efficient and effective networks of social relations, act and speak in ways that build influence, and from an ability to create and employ resources—things that others want and need.

Stop waiting around for bosses and companies to get better and complaining about how are you treated. Build the skills—and use them—that will permit you to create the environment in which you want to live.

Jeffrey Pfeffer is a professor at Stanford Business School and author of *Power: How to Get It, Use It, and Keep It.*

harmony

The word harmony carries some serious baggage. Soft, namby-pamby, liberal, weak. Men who value harmony aren't considered macho. Women who value harmony are considered stereotypical. Success is typically defined with words like hard-(sell, line, ass). Successful people are lauded for being argumentative, self-interested, disruptive. But those assumptions are the dregs of a culture that celebrates the lone hero who leads with singular ambition all the while damning the sheep who follow him in harmonious ignorance.

No.

Harmony is a springboard. Harmony supports teamwork. And teamwork creates energy. An energy that fuels creativity. When focusing on harmony, success becomes defined by different terms. Contribution. Dedication. Cooperation.

Harmony takes bravery, an open heart. It takes lying awake at night when one of your co-workers is having a rough patch and dreaming up ways to help.

In the true sense of karma, to achieve harmony, you must always do the right thing with no eye on a reward. The reward will come because there is trust on the other side.

Harmony creates a workplace where you and all the people around you love to be.

Jack Covert is the head honcho at 800ceoread. **Sally Haldorson** is the company's resident wordsmith.

tough-mindedness

We live in the age of distraction, of Twitter and multi-tasking and short attention spans. Even these micro-essays are part of it. Whereas what produces real work (and happiness for each of us, in my opinion) is depth, focus, concentration and commitment over time.

The antidote to these scattering influences is tough-mindedness, which I define as the ability to draw lines and boundaries within which we protect and preserve the mental and emotional space to do our work and to be true to our selves. Not to the point of insanity (we gotta keep a sense of humor about this stuff), but we also desperately need the ability to play real hard-ball with ourselves when we need it. Otherwise, we'll all expire from sheer shallowness. I've written about showing up in my "Writing Wednesday's" series, drawing examples from Patricia Ryan Madson's book *Improv Wisdom*. There's tremendous power in putting your ass where your heart wants to be. Being there is just the first step. You must stay for more than a few minutes or one 140-character post.

Special Forces Major Jim Gant wrote the seminal report "One Tribe At A Time". He's a husband and father, who was training for a one-year deployment to Iraq at the time, while also juggling the everyday issues we all face. No one asked him to write the paper. Conviction, passion and a dedication to hard work were on his side – that's tough-mindedness.

Steven Pressfield is the author of *Gates of Fire* and *The War of Art*. He blogs at "It's the Tribes, Stupid." (blog.stevenpressfield.com)

evangelism

The future belongs to people who can spread ideas. Here are ten things to remember:

1. Create a cause. A cause seizes the moral high ground and makes people's lives better.
2. Love the cause. "Evangelist" isn't a job title. It's a way of life. If you don't love a cause, you can't evangelize it.
3. Look for agnostics, ignore atheists. It's too hard to convert people who deny your cause. Look for people who are supportive or neutral instead.
4. Localize the pain. Never describe your cause by using bull shiitake terms like "revolutionary" and "paradigm shifting." Instead, explain how it helps a person.
5. Let people test drive the cause. Let people try your cause, take it home, download it, and then decide if it's right for them.
6. Learn to give a demo. A person simply cannot evangelize a product if she cannot demo it.
7. Provide a safe first step. Don't put up any big hurdles in the beginning of the process. The path to adopting a cause needs a slippery slope.
8. Ignore pedigrees. Don't focus on the people with big titles and big reputations. Help anyone who can help you.
9. Never tell a lie. Credibility is everything for an evangelist. Tell the truth—even if it hurts. Actually, especially if it hurts.
10. Remember your friends. Be nice to the people on the way up because you might see them again on the way down.

Guy Kawasaki is a founding partner and entrepreneur-in-residence at Garage Technology Ventures. He is also the co-founder of Alltop.com. Previously, he was an Apple Fellow at Apple Computer, Inc. Guy is the author of nine books.

compassion

"It's nothing personal, it's just business." We spend more than 50% of our lives at work. Why would anyone want to wake up in the morning and go to work with that attitude? If you don't make it personal, and if you don't make it count, what's the point? Business is missing one important core value: compassion. "Between work and family, I have no time for community."

This is something everyone feels at some point in their lives. But think about it: What if we made community an integral part of our business? What if we recognized that we can't have strong businesses without a strong community and we can't have a strong community without compassion?

The real way strong communities are built is through the compassion we extend to others. Both to those we know, and to those we don't know. The Internet is amazing because it connects us all. Compassion for those around us now extends globally and beyond our physical boundaries. We can all do more for each other and be better. Be compassionate to everyone no matter the level of connection. Make compassion a core business value. Start with a smile to a stranger. Start by getting others to nod in agreement when you say: "If we're not compassionate to one another, what's the point in the end?"

Mitch Joel is President of Twist Image and author of *Six Pixels of Separation*.

knowledge

How does news shape the way we see the world? Distorted, bloated, and not representative of what is happening.

Too often, American commercial news is myopic and inwardly focused. This leads to a severe lack of global news. And increasingly, a shortage of "enterprise journalism" – journalistic depth built over time through original sources – that provides the context and enables thoughtful response.

Too often, the news sticks to crime, disasters, infotainment, and horse-race politics. Many important topics such as education, race and ethnicity, science, environment, and women and children's issues are often less than 5% of all news combined.

Much of widely-seen online news isn't better – it's often just re-circulates the same stories.

The result: much of our news can't be called "knowledge media" – content that builds insight about our world.

It's difficult to understand the world, if you haven't heard much about it. But we also know many Americans want to know more.

Storytelling is powerful. It helps us understand, make choices and can inspire us.

Journalism as we know it is in trouble. The old models don't serve us anymore with the content we need. Now is our chance to make it better.

By investing aggressively and entrepreneurially in the future of knowledge media – in both journalistic reportage and in powerful storytelling, we can ensure that people get the fullest global perspective. The Time is Now.

Alisa Miller is the President & CEO of PRI, Public Radio International, and her new blog is Global Matters Post.

parsing

How many times have you paid your taxes? Ever get a receipt back telling you what you bought? You're paying for something, right? Why is everybody arguing about taxes and deficits when they don't know how their money is being spent?

What if you went to Lowe's, and paid to improve your home, then Lowe's did work but didn't tell you what they did. Would you notice if they fixed faulty wiring?

It is time for us to rationalize the debate. Let's parse the data and free the facts. Imagine if we organized around meaningful data instead of vapid rhetoric. What if you could see how much you spent on your commute to work this year, or defending your country, or keeping your neighbor healthy? What if there was as much data about John Barrow (D-GA) as there was about Manny Ramirez (LF-Dodgers). There are 750 players in Major League Baseball, and only 535 Members of Congress. Most of the data exists and what doesn't we need to demand.

The answer to healthy democracy lies not in rhetoric, but in our data. That's parsing I can believe in.

Clay Johnson is the Director of Sunlight Labs for the Sunlight Foundation. He tweets at @cjoh.

forever

You are immortal. The result of everything you do today will last forever. Everything you buy, own, consume is likely to last forever somewhere in a landfill. Even the majority of the the recyclable materials you use will not be processed and these 'green' items will be found piled up in deep far-off valleys whether you like it or not.

When our great great grandchildren finally work out how to solve the selfish errors of our time, we will be considered primitive: our balance with our habitat ignored in pursuit of progress. But as humans we strive for progress. We will not live alone self sufficiently on our rural hectare and therefore we must bring simple common sense to everything we buy, own and consume.

If they will last forever, then we must make these items as useful as they can be for as long as possible. Products needs to be kept, repaired, loaned and shared. Packaging needs to be reused and returned. That is progress. Yes, the future will have smaller markets but tomorrow's business leaders will be the first ones to build markets today that have a focus on forever.

Piers Fawkes inspires his PSFK.com readers, event attendees and corporate clients to make things better. His latest click to print book is *Good Ideas in 2010*.

empathy

Our word is dangerously polarized. There is an imbalance of wealth and power that has resulted in widespread alienation, suspicion, and resentment. Yet we are linked together more closely than ever before – electronically, politically, and economically.

One of the most important tasks of our generation is to build a just and viable global order, where all peoples can live together in mutual respect. We have it in our power to begin the world again by implementing the ancient principle that is often called the Golden Rule: Always treat all others as you would wish to be treated yourself. We need to make this compassionate and empathic ethos a vibrant force in private and public life, developing a global democracy, where all voices are heard, working tirelessly and practically for the well-being of the entire human race, and countering the dangerous mythology of hatred and fear.

At this crossroads of history, we have a choice. We can either emphasize the exclusive and chauvinist elements that are found in all our traditions, religious or secular or those that teach us to celebrate the profound interdependence and unanimity of the human race.

Karen Armstrong is a bestselling author, winner of 2008 TED prize and creator of the Charter for Compassion.

neoteny

Neoteny is the retention of childlike attributes in adulthood. Human beings are younger longer than any other creature on earth, taking almost twenty years until we become adults. While we retain many our childlike attributes into adulthood most of us stop playing when we become adults and focus on work.

When we are young, we learn, we socialize, we play, we experiment, we are curious, we feel wonder, we feel joy, we change, we grow, we imagine, we hope.

In adulthood, we are serious, we produce, we focus, we fight, we protect and we believe in things strongly.

The future of the planet is becoming less about being efficient, producing more stuff and protecting our turf and more about working together, embracing change and being creative.

We live in an age where people are starving in the midst of abundance and our greatest enemy is our own testosterone driven urge to control our territory and our environments.

It's time we listened to children and allow neoteny to guide us beyond the rigid frameworks and dogma created by adults.

Joichi Ito is the CEO of Creative Commons, blogs at Joi Ito's Web (joi.ito.com), and is an Internet entrepreneur and early stage investor.

celebrate

As I write this, all day long, it's my birthday. I've gotten emails and tweets and Facebook wishes from friends. And I'm grateful to know they're all thinking of me.

But what about the companies and products and services I have relationships with? Why aren't they taking this perfect, regular, anticipated, ego-full chance to single me out from the crowd and make me think of them on my birthday? (Tactics aside…)

Why doesn't iTunes send you a code for 1 free 99-cent song on your birthday?

What if Dunkin Donuts gave you free coffee on your birthday, in a special birthday cup that people will notice (and remark on) when you walk in to the office? Imagine if GoDaddy offered you, Birthday Girl, any 1 of these 10 available variations of your name, today only, for 1 year, free.

What if Twitter put a cupcake icon on your profile. Click and see a live list of everyone who said "Happy Birthday @neilhimself!" that day. It's not just about free stuff and attention from followers. It's about a business making up their minds to have an ongoing relationship with you, to invent fun ways to delight you, and mostly about following through in a way you'll tell your friends about.

Happy birthday.

Megan Casey is Editor in Chief of Squidoo.com

diy

Do it yourself.

Most doctors prescribe pills, I prescribe empowerment. We spend less than an hour per year with our doctor—and 8,765 without. Fortunately, we live in the age of DIY. And now we have the tools to create a new health experience. Dr. Google is always there for us. We can connect with the 500 people in the country all living with the same rare illness. We can email our doctor or meet them by video chat. We can find the nearest farmer's market with our iPhone. We can use the web to find fellow runners in our neighborhood.

Living healthy is getting easier every day. Imagine if your doctor, acting as your consultant, prescribed all these tools for you to be the most empowered CEO of your health. What if you paid your doctor for advice to keep you out of their office? What if we looked at protecting our own health the same way we look at protecting the environment? What if being healthy became a social, not just a personal, cause? Empowerment is the best prevention. My prescription:

Rx: Your health is up to you. Start small. Eat well. Eat less. Move your body. Love your lover. Be a good friend. Let others care about you. Say you're sorry. Laugh a ton. Drink one (sometimes two) for me. Simplify. Buy more experiences than things. Create your health. Do-it-yourself.

Jay Parkinson is co-founder of Hello Health and founding partner in Future Well, a new design firm architecting innovations in health and wellness.

adventure

I've been thinking about how big our world is and how small-minded we've become; how quick we are to judge and how slow to understand.

Technology places the resources of the world at our fingertips, yet we have trouble seeing past the ends of our noses. For every trend there's a counter-trend worth considering. Resolve to leave the screens of your virtual world momentarily behind, and indulge your senses with a real world adventure. St. Augustine said: "The world is a book, and those who don't travel read only one page."

My advice? Adventure calls. Blaze a new trail. Cross a continent. Dare to discover. Escape the routine. Find a fresh perspective. Go slow; gaze absentmindedly and savor every moment. Have some fun! Invest now in future memories. Journeys are the midwives of thought; Keep a journal. Leave prejudice and narrow mindedness behind. Make for the horizon and meet new people. Navigate the unknown. Observe, and open your mind. Pursue a road less traveled. Quest for truth. Rely on yourself. Sail away from the safe harbor; Take a risk. Unleash your curiosity. Venture further. Why wait? Expect the unexpected. Say Yes to adventure.... journey with Zeal!

Robyn Waters is an Ambassador of Trend, a Champion of Design, and a Cheerleader of Possibilities. She's the author of *The Trendmaster's Guide*.

dumb

A long time ago, starting a company that made software for computers was dumb. Microsoft and Apple may beg to differ. A company that manufactures cars: dumb. Putting a college yearbook online: dumb. Limiting updates to just 140 characters: dumb.

Here's what's easy: to recognize a really smart new business concept as just that. What's hard is recognizing that the idea you think is just plain dumb is really tomorrow's huge breakthrough. But what makes dumb, smart? The ability to look at the world through a different lens from everyone else. To ignore rules. To disregard the 'why's' and 'how's' and 'never-succeeded-befores'.

Then you need conviction, and the ability to stand by that conviction when other (smart) people look you in the eye and say, "no way, nuh uh." So, how do you tell a good dumb idea from a bad dumb one? Good dumb ideas create polarization. Some people will get it immediately and shower it with praise and affection. Others will say it's ignorant and impossible and run for the hills. The fiercer the polarization, the smarter your dumb idea.

Of course, dumb can be just dumb. You just have to be smart to tell the difference.

Dave Balter is a serial entrepreneur and most recently founder and CEO of BzzAgent. He's written two books, *Grapevine: Why Buzz Was a Fad but Word of Mouth is Forever* and *The Word of Mouth Manual: Volume II*.

nobody

Nobody has the answers.
Nobody is listening to you.
Nobody is looking out for your interests.
Nobody will lower your taxes.
Nobody will fix the education system.
Nobody knows what he is doing in Washington.
Nobody will make us energy independent.
Nobody will cut government waste.
Nobody will clean up the environment.
Nobody will protect us against terrorist threats.
Nobody will tell the truth.
Nobody will avoid conflicts of interest.
Nobody will restore ethical behavior to the White House.
Nobody will get us out of Afghanistan.
Nobody understands farm subsidies.
Nobody will spend your tax dollars wisely.
Nobody feels your pain.
Nobody wants to give peace a chance.
Nobody predicted the Iraq War would be a disaster.
Nobody expected the levees to fail.
Nobody warned that the housing bubble would collapse.
Nobody will reform Wall Street.
Nobody will stand up for what's right.
Nobody will be your voice.
Nobody will tell you what the others won't.
Nobody has a handle on this.
Nobody, but you, that is.
Never forget, a small group of people can change the world.
No one else ever has.

Micah Sifry is co-founder of the Personal Democracy Forum. He tweets @mlsif.

analog

Analog computing, once believed to be as extinct as the differential analyzer, has returned. Digital computing can answer (almost) any question that can be stated precisely in language that a computer can understand. This leaves a vast range of real-world problems—especially ambiguous ones—in the analog domain.

In an age of all things digital, who dares mention analog by name? "Web 2.0" is our code word for the analog increasingly supervening upon the digital—reversing how digital logic was embodied by analog components, the first time around.

Complex networks—of molecules, people, or ideas—constitute their own simplest behavioral descriptions. They are more easily approximated by analogy than defined by algorithmic code. Facebook, for example, although running on digital computers, constitutes an analog computer whose correspondence to the underlying network of human relationships now drives those relationships, the same way Google's statistical approximation to meaning—allowing answers to find the questions, rather than the other way around—is now more a landscape than a map.

Pulse-frequency coding (where meaning is embodied by the statistical properties of connections between memory locations) and template-based addressing (where data structures are addressed by template rather than by precise numerical and temporal coordinates) are the means by which the analog will proliferate upon the digital. Analog is back, and here to stay.

George Dyson is the author of *Baidarka*, *Project Orion* and *Darwin Among the Machines*, as well as a recent short story, "Engineers' Dreams."

independent diplomacy

It's a cliché that we are all now subject to cross-border forces. States and governments are less and less able to control the things that affect our lives. How should we manage?

I was once a British diplomat. I believed that governments understood – and controlled - everything, and that diplomacy could deal with our new challenges. I was wrong. Diplomacy has not evolved to deal with new threats and the range of people and groups who shape the world.

I resigned over Iraq. I had been Britain's Iraq expert at the UN for several years. I knew that my government had manipulated the evidence to sell an invasion to which there were better alternatives. I then worked for Kosovo, a small country undergoing a transition to statehood, but without the benefit of diplomats. I founded Independent Diplomat to help small countries and political groups engage with and understand the previously closed world of international diplomacy. Everyone involved in the complex problems of our time needs a way to have a say.

What's more, if the world is affected by corporations, NGOs, rock stars and criminal networks - and not only states - this means that everyone has the chance to shape it. But the opportunity is only available to those who act. Everyone can be an independent diplomat. Indeed, everyone may need to be.

Carne Ross is a former senior British diplomat, who founded and heads Independent Diplomat, the world's first non-profit diplomatic advisory group. He authored *Independent Diplomat: Dispatches from an Unaccountable Elite*.

thnx

"Social media" facilitates direct engagement with consumers to an unprecedented level, fundamentally shifting the concept of customer service. No one expected the CEO of Pepsi to ring their doorbell or call on their birthday. It wasn't feasible. But now, the cost of interaction has plummeted. I can thank someone by texting "thnx" from my cell phone between meetings, or hang out on Ustream answering questions, or send an @ reply on Twitter. All at minimal cost.

Every CEO and business must recognize that customer service is now their primary business. What was unreasonable becomes essential; the empowerment of the individual consumer affects every brand.

In this world content creation becomes imperative, the initial engagement. When you are transparent and engaging, the result is what I call the "thank you" economy. I gave away information for free—online videos and keynotes with content similar to my book. Monetizing that scenario sounds difficult but wasn't. People didn't buy 1 book, they bought 4 or 5 copies as a thank you for what they had already received.

I believe the thank you economy will become the norm in 2010 and beyond, and brands that fail to adjust will be left out in the cold.

Gary Vaynerchuk is the author of the New York Times bestselling book, *Crush It! Why Now is the Time to Cash in on your Passion*. He dispenses business advice on his personal blog.

attention

You can **buy** attention (advertising). You can **beg** for attention from the media (public relations). You can **bug** people one at a time to get attention (sales). Or you can earn attention by creating something interesting and valuable and then publishing it online for free: a YouTube video, a blog, a research report, photos, a Twitter stream, an ebook, a Facebook page.

Most organizations have a corporate culture based on one of these approaches to generating attention (examples: Procter & Gamble primarily generates attention through advertising, Apple via PR, EMC via sales, and Zappos via earning attention on the Web). Often, the defining organizational culture is determined because the founder or the CEO has a strong point of view. When the CEO comes up through the sales track, all attention problems are likely to become sales problems.

Chances are that you'll have to work on your boss to get him or her on board with option four. Since most organizations overspend on advertising and sales and underinvest in creating great information online, this effort is well worth your time.

David Meerman Scott is author of *The New Rules of Marketing and PR* a BusinessWeek bestseller now published in 24 languages.

context

When information is evaluated without context—regardless of highly sophisticated analytics, an infinite amount of compute, energy or time, little if any relevance can be established with certainty.

When information is first placed into context with prior observations, relevance can be determined with basic algorithms and insignificant amounts of compute power.

When each new observation builds on earlier observations, context accumulates. Context accumulation improves accuracy over time and leads to an exciting phenomenon whereby more data is faster – much in the same way the last few pieces of the puzzle are as easy as the first few, despite the fact there are more observations in front of you than ever before.

Information in context makes smart systems smarter. When applied to financial services, more fraud is stopped. When applied to health care, patients live longer, and when applied to transportation optimization, cities produce less carbon.

Jeff Jonas, IBM Distinguished Engineer, Chief Scientist, IBM Entity Analytics. He has a blog at jeffjonas.typepad.com.

change

A troubled teenager named Bobby was sent to see his high-school counselor, John Murphy. Bobby had been in trouble so many times that he was in danger of being shipped off to a special facility for kids with behavioral problems.

Most counselors would have discussed Bobby's problems with him, but Murphy didn't.

MURPHY: Bobby, are there classes where you don't get in trouble?

BOBBY: I don't get in trouble much in Ms. Smith's class.

MURPHY: What's different about Ms. Smith's class?

Soon Murphy had some concrete answers:

1. Ms. Smith greeted him at the door.
2. She checked to make sure he understood his assignments.
3. She gave him easier work to complete. (His other teachers did none of the three.)

Now Murphy had a roadmap for change. He advised Bobby's other teachers to try these three techniques. And suddenly, Bobby started behaving better.

We're wired to focus on what's not working. But Murphy asked, "What IS working, today, and how can we do more of it?"

You're probably trying to change things at home or at work. Stop agonizing about what's not working. Instead, ask yourself, "What's working well, right now, and how can I do more of it?"

Chip and Dan Heath are the authors of *Made to Stick* and the soon-to-be-released book *Switch: How to Change Things When Change is Hard*.

passion

Some people ask, "What if I haven't found my true passion?" It's dangerous to think in terms of "passion" and "purpose" because they sound like such huge overwhelming ideas.

If you think love needs to look like "Romeo and Juliet", you'll overlook a great relationship that grows slowly. If you think you haven't found your passion yet, you're probably expecting it to be overwhelming.

Instead, just notice what excites you and what scares you on a small moment-to-moment level.

If you find yourself glued to Photoshop, playing around for hours, dive in deeper. Maybe that's your new calling.

If you keep thinking about putting on a conference or being a Hollywood screenwriter, and you find the idea terrifies but intrigues you, it's probably a worthy endeavor for you.

You grow (and thrive!) by doing what excites you and what scares you everyday, not by trying to find your passion.

Derek Sivers is an entrepreneur and programmer. Read sivers.org and try muckwork.com

magnetize

Markets have been through a rough patch lately. But it's time for us to give them a new job to do. The powerful economic forces that have trashed our planet are the only forces powerful enough to save it. So are we doing all we can to put markets to work to drive down global warming pollution—the most serious environmental problem—while there's still time?

We need to magnetize ourselves. Markets, acting like a magnet, create a pull on people and businesses. So when a market is designed to protect the environment, it attracts brainpower and capital toward green solutions, aligning private incentives with the public good. It's all about getting the rules right.

The global warming crisis, like the recent turmoil in the financial system, shows why we need to design markets well and regulate risks appropriately. A worldwide carbon market will combat global warming by pulling inventors and investors—and you and me and everyone—toward low-carbon energy solutions.

Markets can unleash people's creativity, guide entrepreneurs and catalyze innovation. By harnessing markets to protect the environment, we can align human aspirations with planetary needs—and save ourselves from ourselves.

Fred Krupp is president of Environmental Defense Fund and coauthor with Miriam Horn of *Earth: The Sequel*, the New York Times bestseller on low-carbon energy inventions. He's on Twitter.

confidence

Confidence is rocket fuel for your business life. Confident people have a come-this-way charisma that generates a following. When you possess total confidence you are willing to take risks. When you have it, you propel yourself and your team forward into the future.

Problem: Most people don't cultivate confidence – it just lands on them due to favorable conditions. I call this spot confidence. Good times make for confident people. Bad times crush them, along with their daring point of view.

The secret to unbreakable confidence is a lifestyle of emotional/mental diet and exercise.

1. **Feed Your Mind Good Stuff.** Stop reading negative information, listening to negative people or watching cable network news. You are loading up with fear. Replace that information with studies about the future or an improved you. You'll soon emerge as a solution provider instead of a Chicken Little.

2. **Exercise Your Gratitude Muscle.** Gratefulness is a muscle, not a feeling. You need to work it out daily. Every morning, give thanks to two people that helped you yesterday and one person that will assist you today. This will focus your mind on what you have, and you'll soon realize you are not alone.

Tim Sanders, author of Love Is The Killer App: How To Win Business & Influence Friends. You can follow him on Twitter.

slow capital

I've spent almost twenty-five years in the capital markets watching investors behave. Way too often it is a "wham bam" experience and then off to the next deal. Things like exploding offers, "fly by" board members, and shotgun marriages are so common that you sometimes wonder how anyone makes any money.

We need to embrace "slow capital." Here are some basic tenets:

1. Slow capital doesn't rush to conclusions and doesn't expect entrepreneurs to do so either

2. Slow capital flows into a company based on the company's needs, not the investor's needs

3. Slow capital starts small and grows with the company as it grows

4. Slow capital has no set timetable for getting liquid: slow capital is patient capital

5. Slow capital takes the time to understand the company and the people who make it up

---

Fred Wilson is Managing Partner, Union Square Ventures. You can read his blog (avc.com) and follow him on Twitter.

open-source dna

99.99% of the code in your cells is also in mine. We are 99.99% identical. There are very few genes that are unique to you. Probably none. The same can be said of our faces. But what our faces portray is the unique combination, or arrangement of very common parts. Humans have an uncanny ability to distinguish the less than .01% difference among faces and declare them unique. So we talk about "our" face, even though we share most, if not all of it with others in our extended family. To species outside of humans we probably look like identical penguins.

This means that just as computers make regulation of the press and the control of copies impossible, computers embedded in DNA-tricorder devices will make regulation of DNA sequencing as impossible to control. Anyone will be able to sequence anything they want.

Eventually, the cost of sequencing will be so cheap, that it will become mandatory for certain purposes. For instance, thousands of effective therapeutic medicines today cannot be sold because they induce toxic side effects in some people. Sometimes the sensitive will share a cluster of genes. If this group can be excluded using gene testing, the otherwise effective medicine can be prescribed to the rest. Several drugs on the market today already require genetic screening for this purpose.

There will surely be people who will not share any part of their genome with anyone under any circumstances. That's okay. But great benefits will accrue to those who are willing to share their genome. By making their biological source code open, a person allows others to "work" on their kernel, to mutually find and remedy bugs, to share investigations into rare bits, to pool behavior results, to identify cohorts and ancestor codes. Since 99.99% of the bits are shared, why not?

It will become clear to those practicing open-source personal genomics that genes are not destiny; they are our common wealth.

Kevin Kelly has seen our future. He is involved in the Long Now Foundation and Wired Magazine. Kevin is the author of several essential books and blogs.

technology

For those of us who have a hand in building technology-based products, we often focus on achieving business-defined success metrics without considering the impact of what we don't (or can't) measure. Here are some notable themes in technology to reflect upon the consequences of what we're creating when we design.

Legacy: "Legacy" used to mean the stuff of legend. Nowadays, in technology, it's the outdated stuff that no one wants to inherit or support. Not too long ago, we designed for disposability, planned obsolescence, and cost reduction by all means necessary. Now, we have garbage dumps piled high with the unwanted and unsafe consequence of products that don't degrade and were born out of caprice. Good design always stems from an understanding of the context you're designing for—we just need to acknowledge that our contextual accountability extends beyond what's explicitly defined for us in a spec. As technology makes it cheap and easy to release products simply to see what happens, it's important to remember that the rest of the world shouldn't be expected to inherit and clean up someone else's shortsighted spec.

Design for a humanist experience: Technology has a reputation for making us feel stupid, helpless, less human. Designing technology for a humanist experience changes that. Take Kacie Kinzer's innovative Tweenbots—robots that require human intervention in order to reach their goal. Or Foursquare—a location-based application for discovering places and socializing with your friends in physical space. Instead of simply using technology to supplant us for the things we're not so good at, humanist design lets us do what we do best: It lets humans be human. It's a great reminder that, when designed thoughtfully, our experiences with technology don't need to be wholly outsourced to the point where we lose our sense of being.

Phoebe Espiritu is a design problem-solver with a master's from NYU's Interactive Telecommunications Program (ITP.) She's working on fundraising for ITP's Red Burns Scholarship Fund

expertise

Expertise is typically over-rated. Sometimes you have to rely on feedback to grow.

My first SEO website had a serious error which earned me a chastising email, which at that the time didn't feel so good. I responded to his email and fixed the error and today, the sender does not remember writing that email and has a big promotion for my site on his website. If you care and are receptive to feedback appropriately, eventually the market will help sort things out for you. People will come across your work and suggest helpful tools and ideas. Some will be rude, some will be condescending, and some will be generous and kind.

But if you keep everything in your head then you can't expect anyone else to appreciate your genius or trust your knowledge - they don't know it exists.

Ignorance can be an advantage, and feedback an incredibly useful tool. It allows you to share the journey, which helps make writing accessible to beginners. And it allows you the courage to do things you would not do if you waited until you already knew everything, especially because as you learn more, you learn how much you don't know.

Aaron Wall writes SEO Book, a website about the ever-changing world of search. He is also authoring a book by the same name.

fascination

Why, exactly, do humans smile? This question puzzled anthropologists for hundreds of years. The smile is instinctive, one of a thousand fascination cues we use to persuade others to connect with us. Yet from an evolutionary perspective, the smile makes no sense. In the animal kingdom, retracting the mouth corners and baring teeth is a sign of aggression. Yet in humans, this same gesture signals openness. {So why are humans different?} The answer: Bigger animals have bigger mouths, and therefore lower vocal vibrations, which conveys dominance. Smaller animals have smaller mouth cavities, and their higher voices communicate friendliness or submission. It's why a Rottweiler's growl is more threatening than a Pomeranian's.*

When humans smile, we pull our cheek flesh back against our teeth, which makes our mouth cavity smaller, and raises the pitch of our voice. Presto, we sound friendlier essentially turning ourselves from a big animal into a smaller one. Smiling, anthropologists realized, began as a way to sound less threatening then evolved into a way to look more approachable. The next time you become captivated by a person (or a brand or idea), without even realizing it, you're most likely under the influence of the fascination triggers.

* Humans have a hardwired connection between pitch of voice and facial expression. A simple experiment: Sing the highest note that you're capable of, and notice how you raise your chin and eyebrows (almost like you're cooing to a baby). Then, sing the lowest note. See how your chin and eyebrows lower, in a more aggressive expression?

Sally Hogshead is a speaker, brand consultant, and author of the upcoming book, *FASCINATE: Your 7 Triggers to Persuasion and Captivation*.

difference

For 2,500 years in the West, we've tried to settle matters, because that's what it meant to know something. Hyperlinks have revealed that that's really just a result of using paper to codify knowledge: Books settle matters because they're self-contained, fundamentally disconnected from other books, written by a relative handful of people, and impossible to change after they are printed. So, our basic strategy for knowing has been to resolve differences and move on: There's only one right answer, and once it's known, we write it down, and go on to the next question.

That works fine for a small class of factual information. But, much of what we want to understand is too big, complex, and arguable to ever be settled.

The hyperlinked world—the Web—is made for this way of networked knowing. A hyperlinked world includes all differences and disagreements, and connects them to one another. We are all smarter for having these differences only a click away. The challenge now is to learn how to evaluate, incorporate, respect, and learn from them. If we listen only to those who are like us, we will squander the great opportunity before us: To live together peacefully in a world of unresolved differences.

David Weinberger is a Senior Researcher at the Harvard Berkman Center for Internet & Society. He blogs at Joho the blog (hyperorg.com).

world-healers

All traditional cultures recognize certain people as natural-born mystical healers (shamans, medicine men, pick your label). Modern Western culture has no category for such people. But that doesn't mean they aren't here. Right now, everywhere, ordinary people born to the archetype of the shaman are feeling compelled to begin finding one another and fulfilling their inborn purpose.

The great challenge of the 21st century is to wage peace on a globe full of humans while repairing the unintended damage we've inflicted on ourselves, other beings, and the earth. We need modern shamans to channel ancient "technologies of magic" like empathy, creativity, art, and spiritual interconnection, through "magical technologies" like medicine, computers, and satellites. That marriage of ancient and cutting-edge genius can heal hearts, minds, beasts, plants, ecosystems—almost anything. If you feel something stirring in your heart at the thought that you may be shaman-born, pay attention. This is not an accident. Some as-yet unexplained force is calling you to join in a healing of unprecedented scope. And though that healing will, of course, follow the laws of science, doing it will feel like pure magic.

Martha Beck, Ph.D., is a coach, writer, and columnist for O, the Oprah Magazine.

sacrifice

A winning business understands that to **gain** a customer it must first be willing to **lose** a customer. Unfortunately, we've been conditioned to do whatever it takes to not lose a customer. To always say YES to customers. To always kowtow to the whims of customers. That's unfortunate because winning companies are willing to sacrifice losing customers to win customers.

American Apparel wins customers by losing customers. Its provocative advertising and strong stance on political issues offends some consumers. American Apparel sacrifices appealing to everybody to only appeal to select somebodies who appreciate the brand's unique personality.

Costco wins customers by losing customers. Its membership model shuns consumers not willing to pay the yearly membership fee. Its broad but shallow merchandise mix turns off consumers wanting more choices. Costco makes deliberate sacrifices because its customers will also make deliberate sacrifices in exchange for lower prices.

Winning businesses have a common trait, an obvious and divisive point of view. Losing businesses also have a common trait, a boring personality alienating no one and thus, sparking passion from no one. Is your business designed to be a winning business? Is your business willing to sacrifice losing customers to win customers?

John Moore is a marketingologist; he operates the Brand Autopsy Marketing Practice.

focus

"Focus. Most important." That's what Mr. Miyagi said.

For Daniel-san, his attention was scattered. Thoughts of moving to Fresno consumed him and his sensei was teaching a simple lesson in self-control.

In business, too, we struggle to obtain focus. More is better, seems the implied message. Our instinct nudges us toward a scattershot approach, because we fear missing an untried path. Like the Karate Kid, we need to practice our own self-control.

Many mentors beyond Miyagi have advised us on the benefits of focus. Jim Collins tells us to be a hedgehog and find our singular purpose. Al Ries and Jack Trout have always said to position yourself to own one word. Chris Zook even quantifies the rewards of focus, showing that the top company in any industry captures 70 percent of profits.

In seeing the pixels that make the picture, focus can become a form of inquiry. We notice things we missed. New connections appear. The questions change. Meanings change. When we focus, the answer is always something new.

Be present, the Zen Buddhists say. This is what Mr. Miyagi was saying too.

Todd Sattersten is an author and speaker who blogs at toddsattersten.com.

leap

I always start my fiction-writing classes by telling my students this: "show don't tell." It is the classic rule of writing, to use details, to engage all the senses of the reader by 'showing.' In this way, fiction is like faith. To believe in something is often to be unable to talk about satisfactorily but you can show the manifestations of that belief in your life.

This, I think, is also a good way of looking at our lives, in general.

Show don't tell. To write fiction and to have faith is to take an imaginative leap.

And because life is always full of doubts and fears, to act is to take that leap.

So leap.

Chimamanda Ngozi Adichie is the author of *Half of a Yellow Sun*.

women

We live in a world that is owned by men, designed by men and managed by men, and yet we expect women to participate.

But did you know…

1. Women dominate higher education. Most college and university campuses across North America are 60-40 female.

2. Approximately 70% of all American females work outside the home, and women make up nearly 50% of the total workforce.

3. During the recent recession, 82% of job losses befell men, and mothers are the major breadwinners in 40% of American families.

4. The earning power of women globally is expected to reach $18 trillion by 2014

If you're a man running a business, and if the power and influence females wield hasn't completely registered on your radar, well, then, what we've got here is a failure to communicate.

If your store, restaurant, bank, hotel lobby, mall, or other public space or amenity doesn't acknowledge the female factor; if it doesn't invite women in and make them feel at home, at ease, safe, hygienic, respected and in control, if it doesn't take into account what women want and expect (which is different from what men want and expect), well, then, it's bad business.

Paco Underhill is the CEO of Envirosell and the author of *Why We Buy* and soon to be published *What Women Want*.

timeless

What Would Buddha Tweet?

Here is our paradox. We have never had more communications tools at our disposal, and yet we have never been less effective at communicating

It's human nature to want the shiny new things. The amateur golfer thinks that with that new titanium driver she'll be as good as Tiger Woods. And we believe that social marketing will magically transform our mediocre messages into the word of God.

Like all good Buddhists, I believe that when things become chaotic and complicated, it becomes ever more urgent to cut through the noise, simplify and hone in on what really matters.

Here are three timeless principles of good cause-related communications that will be as important in ten years as they are today: heart, simplicity, and story.

Heart – engage your community from a place of passion and compassion. Facts matter less.

Simplicity – if you can't tell your brand story to a 9-year-old it's no good

Story – the root of all: "Millions survive without love or home, almost none in silence; the opposite of silence leads quickly to narrative, and the sound of story is the dominant sound of our lives…" – Reynolds Price

---

Mark Rovner is founder of Sea Change Strategies, a firm that works with remarkable causes to help them engage the world with passion, vigor, and clarity.

.eDO

The 21st Century challenge for education is to integrate learning into the growing richness of digital life where students are active and engaged every day. The Internet is where they already enjoy autonomy, where they see themselves as doers. Combining cell phones and web services, students are hands-on learners who adapt technology to their own personal uses. They make new connections by sharing their experiences, answering the question: "What are you doing?" They are learning to develop their own social networks. As economist Tyler Cowan points out in his book "Create Your Own Economy," they are already producing real value.

While this increasingly digital culture emerges, there is a resurgence of interest in making things, often called the Do-It-Yourself movement. DIY does not seem to be a reaction against digital life but actually a mashup of physical and virtual worlds, where what you do in real life is reflected in what you do online, and vice versa. Both are realms for creative expression, sharing what you can do as well as the process of doing it.

We are seeing a DIY approach to education that focuses not on where we learn but how we learn. We are re-discovering John Dewey's idea of "learning by doing," which emphasized the primacy of experience over the accumulation of knowledge. "I believe that education is a process of living and not a preparation for future living," he wrote. As students realize that the tools for living are the same for learning, they will naturally expand the range of things they can do.

Dale Dougherty is the founding editor and publisher of Make Magazine and the creator of Maker Faire.

productivity

Getting things done is not the same as making things happen.

You can... reply to email... pay the bills... cross off to-do's... fulfill your obligation... repeat what you heard... go with the flow... anticipate roadblocks... aim for "good enough."

Or you can... organize a community... take a risk... set ambitious goals... give more than you take... change perceptions... forge a new path... create possibility... demand excellence.

Don't worry too much about getting things done.

Make things happen.

Gina Trapani blogs about software and productivity at Smarterware. Her new book, *The Complete Guide to Google Wave*, is available to read online for free.

iterative capital

Financial capital, human capital, intellectual capital and social capital are tremendous resources for entrepreneurship and value creation. But the endowment exponentially supercharging tomorrow's growth investments can best be described as 'iterative capital.' Iterative capital is the best currency in the world for rapidly researching, developing and evolving ideas into innovation.

Iterative capital – not unlike like finance or talent – is a factor of production that's both platform and process for creating 'investable iterations' for designing and building innovative products and services. Iteration is the medium for innovation. Iteration ain't information. Digital media - Microsoft Excel, Catia, Google, Google Sketch-up, JMP, Facebook, Amazon's S3, etc. - empower more people to build more versions – more iterations - of their models, prototypes and simulations per unit time. The bandwidth and velocity of 'versioning' are both exponentially accelerating. Just as niftily, virtual models living as stress-testable bits in Monte Carlo simulations can quickly and cheaply morph into physical prototypes for real-world exploration - and vice versa. In other words, we're stinking rich and getting richer. It gigahertz so good! These trends are innovation's great friends. Value creation's 'schwerpunkt' has shifted from 'bits' to 'its.'

'Its' will be what the sharpest, keenest and most creative entrepreneurs will be investing to invent the future. Just ask Larry or Sergey or Jeff. But never forget that capital is but an input: having a lot of money doesn't make you a smart investor; having access to a bevy of brilliant people doesn't make you a brilliant manager. Similarly, being a wealthy 'iterative capitalist' doesn't inherently guarantee an impressive ROI - Return on Iteration. So how will individuals and institutions creatively leverage this new wealth? Who will be the Warren Buffetts of 'Iterative Capital'?

A researcher at MIT's Sloan School, **Michael Schrage** uses models, prototypes and experiments to explore the behavioral economics of innovation. He is the author of *Serious Play*.

willpower

We love to believe that willpower determines our actions. "If I just try harder," we tell ourselves, "I can lose that last 10 pounds." Or save $200/month. Or improve our time management.

The problem is, it doesn't work.

Willpower is important, of course, but there's more to behavioral change than just trying harder. Think about all the things we know we "should" do: Exercise regularly, eat healthily, max out our retirement accounts, save more, travel, call Mom…

In one study, researchers tried to understand why people weren't investing in their 401(k)s. In the first example, less than 40% of people contributed to their 401(k). But after they made it automatic—in other words, the day you joined, you're automatically contributing a small amount to your 401(k)—enrollment skyrocketed to over 90%. We know we should fill out that paperwork—and it's probably costing us a lot of money to not be investing—but we just can't seem to get around to it.

It turns out we "know" we need to do all kinds of things, but we often need the right defaults—a small nudge—to actually change our behavior. Can you help design the right defaults to help people in pro-social ways?

Ramit Sethi is the author of I Will Teach You To Be Rich. He writes about personal finance, psychology, and entrepreneurship at iwillteachyoutoberich.com.

mesh

Some things are best shared.

There's a change taking place causing people worldwide to reconsider how we relate to the things in our lives as well as our social geography. This realignment has been happening for decades, but the velocity and reach has grown overwhelmingly in the past five years. We've quietly yet dramatically changed our thinking about lifestyle. Quality of life is moving distinctly away from what we own.

Is it the end of ownership as we know it?

One by one, people are realizing that some things are truly best shared. The Mesh is a movement that is taking place all around us and will grow, reform and spread to engage many more of us. It's reshaping how we go to market, who we partner with and how we find new customers. The opportunity is to embrace the Mesh and hopefully to discover how your current or new business can inspire customers in a world where access trumps ownership.

Lisa Gansky is Instigator In Residence and founder of two early web companies (both acquired) and a foundation, lately spotted diving into The Mesh.

enough

Sometimes, I forget to eat lunch. So, 3:30 arrives, and I attack an infant-sized hillock of greasy takeout. I inhale it, scarcely breathing, a condemned man with minutes 'til dawn.

Two minutes after stopping, yes; I feel like I'm going to die. Filled with regret and shrimp-induced torpor, I groan the empty promise of the glutton: "never again." What happened? How'd I miss when I'd had enough?

I wonder the same thing about folks who check for new email every five minutes, follow 5,000 people on Twitter, or try to do anything sane with 500 RSS feeds. **If you're checking for new email every five minutes, that's 24,000 times a year.** Some graze unlimited bowls of information by choice. Others claim it's a necessity of remaining employed, landing sales, or "staying in the loop." Could be. What about you?

How do you know when you've had "enough?"

Not everything, all the time, completely, forever. Just enough. Enough to start, finish, or simply maintain. Unfortunately, foodbabies only appear after it's too late. And, if your satiety's gauged solely by whether the buffet's still open, you're screwed. Like the hypothalamus-damaged rat, you'll eat until you die.

Before the next buffet trip, consider asking, "How do I know what I need to know — just for now?" Then savor every bite.

Merlin Mann is an independent writer, speaker, and broadcaster who's based in San Francisco. He is the author of *Inbox Zero*, published next year by HarperStudio.

(dis)trust

There are some people we should be able to trust without question. Among them are our physicians and the people we authorize to invest our money. We shouldn't have to doubt the motivation behind their decisions because there should be no other motivation than that they will act according to what is in our best interest.

But with the emergence of each new story about dishonesty, betrayal, and conflict of interest, it is apparent that often this is not the case. It's not that they're necessarily bad people, it is more often they're just expected to make ethical decisions under conditions of misaligned incentives.

Physicians have too many ties to pharmaceutical companies and to their own equipment, while investment bankers and traders get the upside but not the downside of their strategies.

If we want to move forward, we must get a handle on how deep these conflicts of interest run so that we can eliminate them. Only then would we be able to take some actions that will rebuild one of the most important public assets we have – trust.

Dan Ariely is author of the bestseller *Predictably Irrational: The Hidden Forces that Shape Our Decisions* & James B. Duke Professor of Behavioral Economics at Duke University.

social skills

I have really bad social skills, so I am constantly noticing how the whole world revolves around social skills. Research that really blows me away is that people would rather work with someone who is incompetent and likable than someone who is a competent jerk. And then I saw that in some cases elite British crew teams will put a weaker, but very likable, rower on a boat because people row faster if they row with people they like.

In my life, I have had to learn social skills one by one, because I have Asperger Syndrome. I learned to smile at jokes even though I'm too literal to understand most of them; I listen to the rhythm of a sentence to know when it's time to laugh. And I learned how to say, "How are you," with the right tone of voice – to express interest – although to be honest, saying that phrase gives me so much anxiety that I never actually say it.

A few years ago I found myself smack in the middle of the recruiting industry. I ended up, somehow, being an expert on how to attract candidates, and an expert on how to present yourself well to employers. At first I thought it was absurd. I've never worked in human resources, and I've never been a recruiter. But then I realized that I'm an expert on the hiring process because it's all about social skills, and I've been studying them my whole life so that I don't look like a freak.

In fact, it's not just getting a job. Or giving a job. Getting or giving anything is about social skills. The world is about being comfortable where you are and making people feel comfortable, and that's what social skills are. What's important is to be kind, and be gracious and do it in ways that make people want to do that for someone else.

Penelope Trunk is the founder of BrazenCareerist.com. Her blog is blog.penelopetrunk.com.

i'm sorry

There's never really a great way to apologize, but there are plenty of terrible ways.

If you're at a coffee shop, and you spill coffee on someone by accident, what do you say? You'll be horrified and say "Oh my god, I'm so sorry!" When you mean it you say you're sorry - it's a primal response. You wouldn't say "Oh my god, I apologize for any inconvenience this may have caused!" But that's exactly how most companies respond when they make a big mistake

Mistakes happen. How you apologize matters. Don't bullshit people - just say "I'm sorry." And mean it.

Jason Fried is a founder of 37signals. He has a blog and is the co-author of Rework.

sleep

America needs to get some sleep. The prevailing culture tells us that nothing succeeds like excess, that working 80 hours a week is better than working 70, that being plugged in 24/7 is expected, and that sleeping less and multi-tasking more are an express elevator to the top. I beg to differ.

There is nothing that negatively affects our mood, our productivity, or our effectiveness more than lack of sleep. For the last few years, ever since I passed out from exhaustion, broke my cheekbone and got five stitches over my eye, I've been working on bringing more balance to my life.

To do this, I've had to learn to unplug and recharge. To trade multi-tasking for uni-tasking and — occasionally — no-tasking. It's left me healthier, happier, and more able to try to make a difference in the world. My eyes have been opened to the value of regularly closing them.

Arianna Huffington is the co-founder and Editor in Chief of the Huffington Post and the author of twelve books.

knowing

**There is no such thing as boring knowledge.
There is only boring presentation.**

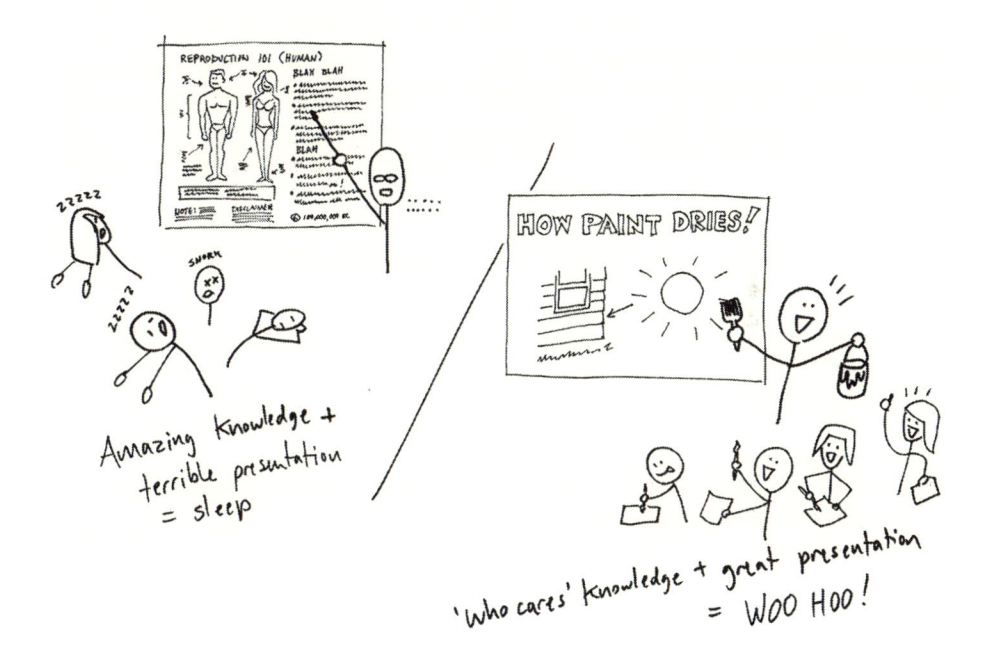

Amazing knowledge + terrible presentation = sleep

'Who cares' knowledge + great presentation = WOO HOO!

Dan Roam solves problems with pictures. He wrote *The Back of the Napkin* and *Unfolding the Napkin*.

government 2.0

Our current government is like a vending machine. We put in taxes, and out come roads, schools, police protection, schools and armies, health care and retirement. And when we don't get the services we want, or the prices are too high, all we can do is shake the vending machine.

Meanwhile, our leaders debate whether to raise prices, and put more goods and services into the vending machine, or to slash prices by reducing the number of offerings.

What if there were another choice? The secret learned by technology providers is to spend less time providing services for citizens, and to spend more time providing services to developers. Every successful technology platform, from the personal computer and the internet to the iPhone, has been profoundly generative: a small investment in open infrastructure that others can build on turns into a vast cornucopia of services.

This is the right way to frame the question of "Government 2.0." How does government become an open platform that allows people inside and outside government to provide better services to each other? In this model, government is a convener and an enabler rather than the first mover of civic action.

> *"When the best leader leads,*
> *the people say 'We did it ourselves.'"*
> – Lao Tzu

Tim O'Reilly is the founder and CEO of O'Reilly Media. He is working to bring together technology and government through his Government 2.0 Summit and Government 2.0 Expo.

gumption

Most of us settle in, and settle for what we have. Rather than pursue, we accept. Our lives become unwitting celebrations of passivity: we undervalue our work and perceive ourselves as wage slaves (and so we phone it in at the day gig), we consume compulsively (but not create), we pine for better lives (but live vicariously through our televisions).

These corners we paint ourselves into, it's no way to live. There's no adventure here, no passion, no hunger for change. Remember that relentless optimism you once had? The goals you wished to achieve, before settling in? They're still there. You need a nudge to find them; a little gumption.

You **can** start that business. You **can** lose that weight. You **can** quit smoking, and learn to garden, and write that book, and be a better parent, and be all the things you want to be ... the thing this world **needs** you to be. It requires courage and faith, both of which you can muster. It requires effort — but this effortless life isn't as satisfying as it seems, is it?

Declare war on passivity. Hush the inner voice that insists you're over the hill, past your prime, unworthy of attaining those dreams. Disbelief is now the enemy, as is the notion of settling. Get hungry — hyena hungry. Get fired up. Find your backbone, and your wings.

Flap 'em. It's the only way you'll be able to fly.

J.C. Hutchins is a novelist. Discover his thriller *7th Son: Descent* at JCHutchins.net.

more people will tell you
that you can't than you can

don't listen

anything's possible

Aimee Johnson, VP Strategic Coffee Initiatives, Starbucks Coffee Company.
Go to www.ted.com for inspiration.

Made in the USA
Lexington, KY
21 May 2012